GUNS N' ROSES

Mark Putterford

OMNIBUS PRESS

Copyright (c) 1993 Omnibus Press
(A Division of Book Sales Limited)

Edited by Chris Charlesworth
Cover & Book designed by 4i Limited
Picture research by David Brolan

ISBN: 0.7119.3217.4
Order No: OP 47192

Exclusive distributors:
Book Sales Limited,
8/9 Frith Street,
London W1V 5TZ, UK.

Music Sales Corporation,
225 Park Avenue South,
New York, NY 10003, USA.

Music Sales Pty Ltd,
120 Rothschild Avenue,
Rosebery, NSW 2018, Australia.

To the Music Trade only:
Music Sales Limited,
8/9 Frith Street,
London W1V 5TZ, UK.

Photo credits:
All Action: 45b; Larry Busacca/Retna: back cover;
George Chin: 5, 9, 15, 24b, 26b, 28, 34t&b, 36b, 45t, 47,
51, 56t&b, 57t, 58t&b, 64t, 69, 70b, 71, 72t&b, 77, 79c,
80c&b, 82, 85t, 88t, 90t; Steve Double: 91; Mitchell
Gerber/Retna: 20; Gene Kirkland/Retna: 10, 11, 12t, 13,
22c, 23, 27, 36t, 37, 42b, 43, 44b, 49t, 50t, 52(x4), 54t&b,
55, 62, 67, 68(x3), 73t&b, 74, 78, 79b, 83, 89t&b, 92,
94t&c, 95; Eddie Malluk/Retna: 16, 26t, 90b; Tony
Mottram/Retna: 14, 29; London Features International:
4t&b, 7, 19, 22t&b, 24t, 25t, 30, 32t, 38t&b, 39, 40, 41,
42t, 44t, 48, 49c&b, 53, 57b, 59, 60, 61, 64b, 65, 66t&b,
68bl, 70t, 75, 76, 81, 84b, 85b, 86, 88b, 96c&b; Neal
Preston/Retna: front cover, 12b, 18, 21, 32b, 35, 56c;
Relay: 2/3, 25r, 31, 46, 79t, 84t, 94b, 96t; Ira
Rosenson/Retna: 28t; Mark Seligar/Retna: 50b; Justin
Thomas/All Action: 17b, 28c, 80t, 87, 93; Ian
Tilton/Retna: 17t, 33; Timothy White/Retna: 8, 63.

Printed and bound in Great Britain by
Scotprint Limited, Musselburgh, Scotland.

Every effort has been made to trace the copyright
holders of the photographs in this book but one or two
were unreachable. We would be grateful if the
photographers concerned would contact us.

A catalogue record for this book is available from the
British Library.

CONTENTS

1   EARLY DAZE

2   THE MUSIC

    APPETITE FOR DESTRUCTION

    LIES

    USE YOUR ILLUSION, PARTS I & II

3   LIFE ON THE ROAD

4   SEX N' DRUGS N' BOOZE

5   WOMEN

6   AXL

7   SLASH

8   IZZY

9   DRUMMERS

10 THE BAND

11 FAME'N'FORTUNE

12 THE FUTURE

13 WHAT OTHERS SAY

EARLY DAZE

When we started we wanted to be
the coolest, sexiest, meanest, nastiest,
loudest, funnest band. There was
a group consciousness of rape,
pillage, search and destroy!
Axl, June 1992

We were a garage band back in Indiana for years, but there was no place to get gigs, unless you talked somebody into renting a hall and you'd do one gig in six months.
Axl, 1987

Everybody's been through the wringer. You go through a lot of bands when you start playing at 15, and in the beginning you don't really know what you want to do. You just want to play. Eventually, you run into each other and the chemistry is just right.
Duff, June 1987

We rehearsed for about two days (for their first tour, the 'Helltour', June 1985). The band was really terrible. There was really no back beat and no soul to it, but the first time we all played together we all knew we had a perfect match of musicians. Stevie (Adler) had a double bass drum and the whole big drum set, and Izzy hid half of his drum set, so all he ended up having was a bass drum, a snare, a floor-tom and some cymbals... We got a car and a U-Haul truck, and we took off with a couple of roadie friends to help us out. Just about 100 miles out of LA our car broke down. The band hitchhiked for about two and a half days to Seattle, because nobody would take us. We were all dressed in our stage clothes - no bags, no luggage, no nothing... five guys in striped, tight pants and boots out in the middle of Oregon. When we finally got there we had to play on other people's equipment, and we were just wasted, and we sucked really badly.

In the meantime, our roadies would try to get the car fixed and meet us in Seattle, and we'd continue the tour. Danny, the driver, had this Union 76 credit card that we were gonna use for all of the gas, because we didn't have any money. Well, he had put the card up in his visor, and when the sun started going on the up side, he flipped the visor over and the wallet went out of the window somewhere. They got stuck, and it took them longer to get back to LA than it did us. We had met this girl who was really cool and gave us a ride all of the way back to LA, and that's about 1300 miles, while our poor roadies were stuck bumming off street corners in different towns all of the way back... We knew that if we could get through that, we could get through anything. It was a real solidifying thing for the band...
Duff, May 1988

... And it just took off from there. There was just like a 'fuck it' attitude. Not 'fuck' in a negative way, just 'fuck it, we're going to play, we're going to do what we're going to do'. After that, you get back to the city and it's like, 'This is a piece of cake!'
Izzy, talking about the same trip, June 1987

When we first started was '85, when the music business was just this big erect monster, it was awful.
Slash, July 1991

We tried to live on $3.75 a day, which was enough to buy biscuits and gravy at Denny's...
Axl, 1986

... You drifted around, you stayed in friends' garages, cars... stayed one step ahead of the sheriffs...
Axl, June 1987

We started out with so many people from so many directions trying to lash out at us.
Axl, 1987

... When we first started out, everybody wanted to hate us. We'd fight promoters tooth and nail just to get a gig. Once we played, people would get really into it. I think they'd be impressed by the fact that we'd just get up there and play.
Slash, February 1991

We just kept playing and we made so much noise in the city, there were so many things happening around us that the labels started to come to us. They came to us! They would come over to the studio and come in the alley and see drunks... there was this drunk with a bottle of Thunderbird on top of his head!... and next thing you know we're going to their office! We made them take us all out for dinner for like a week or two and we started eating good! We'd order all this food and drink and say, 'OK, talk!'
Izzy, June 1987

The buzz got out, and we kept getting invited down to see these idiots. One label... I swear... we were talking to, I was saying, 'It kind of sounds like Steven Tyler', and this chick said, 'Steven who?', and all of us just looked at each other and said, 'Can we have another of those drinks?'
Slash, June 1987

The only door that opened for us was this one guy who saw us and signed us to Geffen. The

We had no money but we could dig up a buck to go down to this liquor store. It happened to sell this great wine called Nightrain that would fuck you up for a dollar. Five dollars and you'd be gone. We lived off this stuff.
Duff, 1987

We didn't have any money, but we had a lot of hangers on and girls we could basically live off. Things were just too easy.
Izzy, 1987

rest was playing live, playing live, playing live. First big tour we did we were opening up for The Cult and nobody knew who the fuck we were, man. We started in Canada and the album wasn't even released. It started with Mötley Crüe, that's when we started to get big. We did it our way, and we didn't compromise our beliefs. And if that opened up some doors and changed around some attitudes in this business, then I'm proud.
Slash, April 1990

Luckily... we never had any money and that's probably why we didn't all kill ourselves back then. None of us had places of our own so we'd walk up and down Hollywood Boulevard and visit every porno store there is, 'cause they stay open 24 hours. We all did various shitty jobs for short periods and that was just to buy drugs or drink 'cause we were so bored and pissed off.

I remember Axl and I once volunteered as medical test subjects for UCLA thinking we'd get pills or something. But it was just a

smoking test and all we got was some free cigarettes. We had to smoke and smoke and we'd get eight bucks an hour for doing that... it was better than nothing.
Slash, June 1992

In the beginning we'd throw parties and ransack the girl's purses while one of the guys was with her.
Axl, 1989

It was like five bags of garbage... all of us in one room and the girls coming over. There was like eight people living there, and a dog. It got really crazy, really crazy. It got really rude. These two girls were like guy-crazy and band-crazy, and there was no way any guy in any band was going to be seen dead with either of them, especially us. So Slash would milk that for everything it was worth... free drinks, free food, everything without ever having to do anything. Which eventually caused big problems...!
Axl, June 1987

So they moved into a studio... No showers, no food, nothing! A very uncomfortable prison cell. But God, did we sound good in there! We're a really loud band and we don't compromise the volume for anything! We'd bash away with a couple of Marshalls in this tiny room, and it was cool because all the losers from Sunset and all the bands would come over and hang out there every night. We used to rehearse in there and sleep in there. But at least we didn't get fat and lazy.

Basically, it's down to a poverty thing, that's where that kind of 'fuck you' attitude comes from, because you're not showering, you're not getting food or nothing, you do what you have to to survive.
Slash, June 1987

For years I was living out of a duffel-bag, and I was happy.
Slash, February 1991

Up until we got signed I lived on the street for five years. I never lived in one place for more than two months, always crashing at people's houses. My parents would say, 'Come back home and go to college and we'll pay for it', but I would reply, 'No, I have to do this for now'.
Axl, 1987

In the beginning our critical acclaim was zero, the industry wanted us dead. There was no support from the business at all. What made us were our shows, 'cause the kids believed in us.
Slash, April 1990

It's like a melting pot, LA. This place was supposed to eat us up; all it did was make us meaner.
Axl, 1987

Izzy and I walked into the Roxy one of our first times and I remember Vince Neil (from Mötley Crüe) and Nikki (Sixx, ditto) leaning over a rail trying to figure out who the fuck we were! It took three years to start getting accepted in LA.
Axl, June 1987

I remember for two years standing at the Troubadour and people wouldn't talk to me.
Axl, June 1987

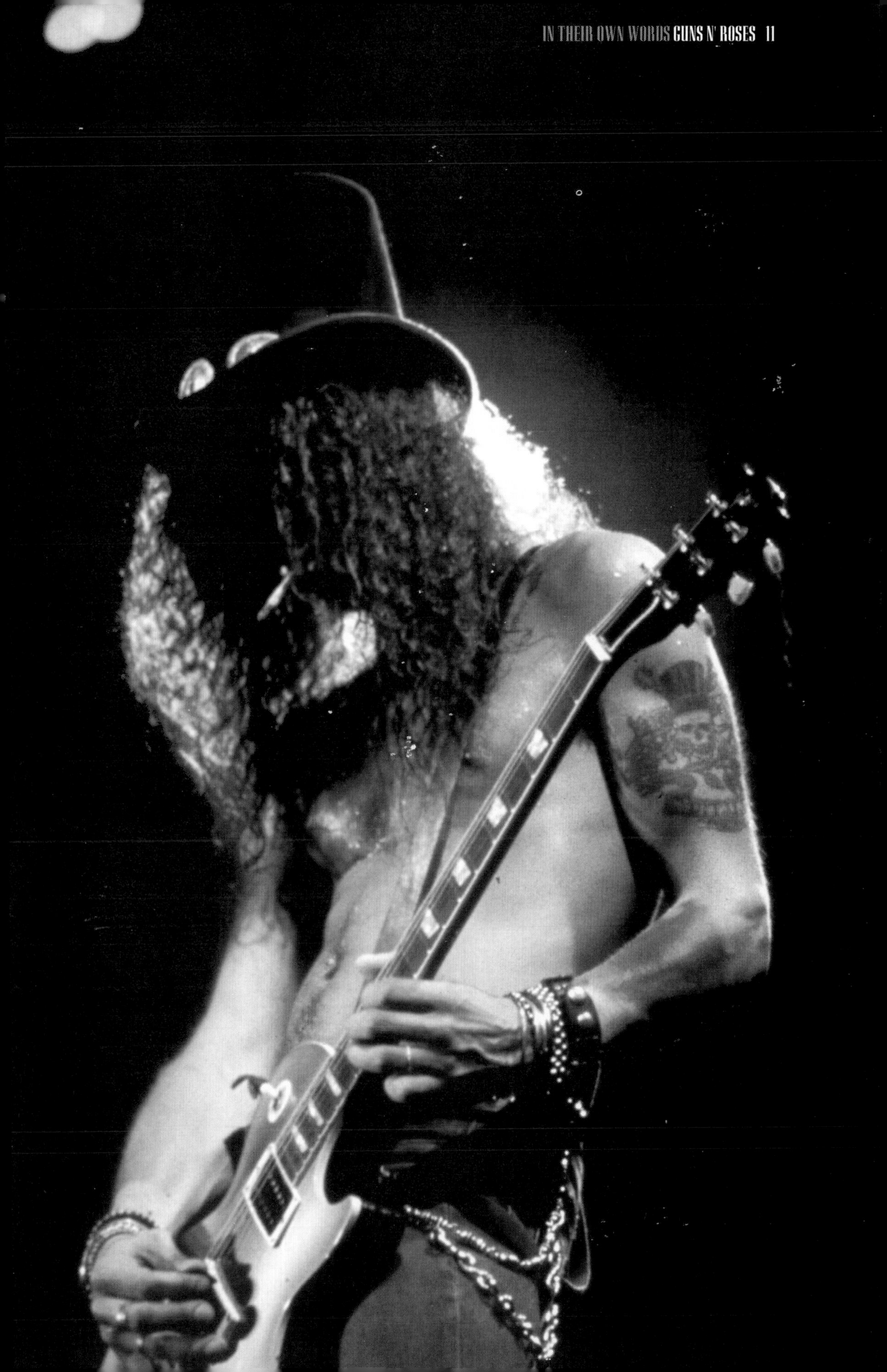

THE MUSIC

I think it's going to kick ass. Listening
to the playback, it's against the
mainstream grain. It's definitely a
case of you'll either love it or hate it...
which is good, as long as you notice it.

Izzy, June 1987

Part I: Appetite For Destruction

There's one song that's kind of like Black Sabbath goes to Ireland...
Axl, June 1987

I want this to be the biggest selling debut album from a rock act ever!
Axl, 1988

We thought we'd made a record that might do as well as, say, Motörhead. It was totally uncommercial. It took a year to even get on the charts! No one wanted to know about it...
Slash, February 1991

I think the only reason it could have gone to No.1 is that we're filling some kind of gap. A gap that hasn't been filled by this particular kind of music for however long it's been. That's the only thing I can attribute it to. It's not because the songs are, like, huge hits. They're not, they're just rock'n'roll songs and fuck the Top Forty, you know? I figure we're just the down and dirty Guns n' Roses band. Everybody wants to have that album because it's not that safe and it looks good next to the George Michael album...
Slash, October 1988

The thing about 'Appetite...' is that it was an album we made because that's what we were all about. It wasn't dictated by industry policy or business decisions, it was an honest record.
Slash, 1990

We were just making a record. Seriously, we didn't think about if it would sell ten copies, never mind one million copies. We didn't know. We didn't really care. We just recorded the music we'd been playing two years before that.
Duff, April 1990

Everybody seems to be doing something completely different, pushing the nice pop single. 'Sweet Child O' Mine' turned into a huge hit and now it makes me sick! I mean, I like it, but I hate what it represents.
Slash, February 1991

I know this girl named Michelle and she became a really good friend of the band's and I was going out with her for a while. I'd written this nice sweet song about her, and then I looked at it and thought, 'That really doesn't touch any basis of reality'. So I put down an honest thing. It describes her life. This girl leads such a crazy life with doing drugs, or

whatever she's doing at the time, you don't know if she's gonna be there tomorrow. Every time I see Michelle I'm really relieved and glad. I showed her the lyrics after about three weeks of debating and she was happy that someone didn't paint just a pretty picture. She loves it. It was a real song about her.

Axl, 1988, explaining the inspiration behind 'My Michelle'

Part II: Lies

It wasn't a follow-up (to 'Appetite For Destruction'). It was only because our first EP ('Live ?!*@ Like A Suicide') was selling for enormous amounts of money in record stores that we released it. If the kids wanted it, we'd give it to them for the right price. And we had some acoustic shit lying around, so we threw that in too.

Duff, April 1990

We did this EP for the same reason as we did the first live EP. It's material that we wanted to get off our chests but without taking up too much space. And it's real simple, real sloppy. You can hear us talking, there's guitar picks dropping. Real off-the-cuff stuff...

Slash, October 1988

There's a line in that song ('One In A Million') where it says, 'Police and niggers, get out of my way...', that I didn't want Axl to sing. I didn't want him to sing that but Axl's the kind of person who will sing whatever it is he feels like singing. So I knew that it was gonna come out and it finally did come out. What that line was supposed to mean, though, was police and niggers, OK, but not necessarily talking about the black race. He wasn't talking about black people so much, he was more or less talking about the sort of street thugs that you run into.

Slash, March 1989

Everybody on the black side of the family was like, 'What's your problem?' My old girlfriend said, 'You could have stopped it'. What am I supposed to say? Axl and I don't stop each other from doing things. Hopefully, if something is really bad, you stop it yourself.

It was something he really wanted to put out to explain his story, which is what the song ('One In A Million') is about. Axl is a naïve white boy from Indiana who came to Hollywood, was brought up in a totally Caucasian society, and it was his way of saying how scared he was and this and that. Maybe somewhere in there he does harbour some sort of (bigoted) feelings because of the way he was brought up. At the same time, it wasn't malicious.

I can't sit here with a clear conscience and say, 'It's OK that it came out'. I don't condone it. But it happened and now Axl is being condemned for it, and he takes it really personally. All I can say, really, is that it's a lesson learned.
Slash, February 1991

The racist thing is just bullshit. I used a word (nigger) that was taboo. And I used that word because it was taboo. I was pissed off about some black people that were trying to rob me. I wanted to insult those particular black people. I didn't want to support rascism. When I used the words 'faggots' I wasn't coming down on gays. I was coming down on an element of gays. I had heard a story about a man who was released out of the LA county jail with AIDS and he was hooking. I've had my fair share of dealings with aggressive gays, and I was bothered by it. The Bible says, 'Thou shalt not judge', and I guess I made a judgement call, and it was an insult. The racist thing, that's just stupid. I can understand how people would think that, but that's not how I meant it...

The most important thing about 'One In A Million' is that it got people to think about racism. A lot of people thought I was talking about entire races or sectors of people. I wasn't. And there was an apology on the record. The apology is not even written that well, but it's on the cover of every record. And no one has acknowledged it yet. No one.
Axl, April 1992

Part III: Use Your Illusion (I & II)

We're gonna go into the studio in, like, October, November...
Slash, June 1988

We'll actually go into pre-production right after we get back from Japan... Some time in the New Year...
Slash, October 1988

Hopefully we'll be into full-blooded pre-production in about a month and a half...
Slash, March 1989

We're definitely, positively, absolutely going to start thinking about considering starting work on the album quite soon... I think.
Izzy, June 1989

We go into the studio on the 15th.
Duff, January 1990

We don't start recording till May 1st.
Axl, January 1990

Looks like we could start recording by the summer.
Slash, February 1990

We're aiming to have the record finished and on the street in time for us to go out on tour again in the summer.
Axl, March 1990

These albums are just so far from me now. Before, when we had it down on tape, it was done. It's gotten to the point now where I don't even ask when they're coming out cos every

We use the same room (at Rumbo Studios, LA), the same producer (Mike Clink)... It's like the 'If the dog doesn't bite you, why kick it in its ass?' theory.
Duff, April 1990

It looks like it's gonna be really good, too. It looks like it's gonna be even more angry and anti-radio and stuff. The first album, everybody was shocked by it 'cos it said 'fuck' on it, like 25 times. This one could be even worse...
Slash, June 1988

time I ask it's a different date. God, it's such a fucking blur. Trying to pin it down is hard, man.
Izzy, October 1991

... I apologise to the kids for taking so long.
Duff, September 1991

There's all kinds of titles for the record... There's, like, 'GN'R Sucks'. That's one of our favourites. There's BUY-Product', like B-U-Y product, like 'Guns n' Roses - BUY Product'...
Axl, January 1990

Anyone who hopes for another 'Appetite For Destruction' is in for a surprise.
Slash, 1990

There's a lot of songs about, you know, drugs and sex.
Slash, February 1991

I'm beginning to come to the realisation that we are kinda in a 'no-win' situation. If we come up with an LP similar to 'Appetite For Destruction' then we'd be heavily criticised for repeating a formula. If, as will be the case, we offer something different then we'll be

attacked for not following 'Appetite...' with something equally as commercial!
Slash, 1990

The biggest thing we had to deal with at one point was like the follow-up thing, right? And we were like, 'Ah fuck, we don't care'. But finally, when we were off the road and it was time to go back in the studio, people were trying to put really heavy pressure on us and we were just like, 'WHAT?!' And it did start turning into pressure. Even (Aerosmith singer) Steven Tyler goes, 'Is there another '...Jungle' on it?' And I was like, 'Of all the people to ask me that!' And at that point we just cut it off from everybody. Y'know, 'We're gonna do OUR record', and that's what we did. If it's successful, it's successful. If it turns out to be a big disappointment... well, I know the band's really proud of it and that's the only thing that's important. It's like, if you want us to do another '...Jungle', why? We did it already...
Slash, August 1991

The new album is so diverse, and it's gone to extremes that we haven't really communicated to the people who listen to us.

Maybe in concert we've come close to it. It's a lot heavier in concert than the 'Appetite...' album. We seem to be extreme in two ways. It's really heavy, or really mellow. There's acoustics and horns and shit like that...
Slash, April 1990

I don't think there are any singles on the record.
Slash, 1991

We call it ('November Rain') our 'Layla' song.
Slash, February 1991

This record is heavy, but even in the heavy tracks there's something else. It's all very varied. All you have to do is just listen to it. If you like it, you like it; if you don't, you don't. We did it and that's that.
Slash, June 1991

We wanted to record all our new material, go back and clean the slate of all the old material that we never got a chance to record before... Just get it all off our chests so that when we started the next one there'd be nothing lingering.
Slash, September 1991

I think diehard Guns fans don't expect anything in particular. That's what makes them diehard. The people whom we'll surprise the most are the fucking critics who like to fuck with people. They'll try to take this album apart and shit. They'll analyse it. But the fans will know what's going on.
Duff, April 1990

A lot of the material was written while we were going through these emotional or personal transitions, as well as those chemical situations.
Slash, 1991

The whole point of doing it as two seperate albums is, number one, a double album's going to cost a kid, what, 25 or 30 bucks? A young kid can't really afford that, so he and his friend can go out and buy one record each, and tape the other one. Also, it's never been done before, and you know us, we like to try shit that's never been done. It's just a funny idea to fuck with the system. It might work, it might flop. I know the critics are looking for the things to flop, but I know it won't because I'm big-headed, because I love our material, and because our heart and blood, everything is in there.
Duff, September 1991

One thing about this album is that a lot of these songs were written during different time periods for us... some of them even before we met one another. So what happens is, you have lyrics to a song and some music that one of the other guys wrote a long time ago, and you go in to record it, and you can't catch the vibe of whatever he was feeling at the time he wrote it.
Slash, June 1991

'Use Your Illusion' is also very ironic for us. I mean, I don't know why but this band has just generated bullshit hype for so long that it's like throwing it back in their faces. And d'you know what? The album is so controversial. It's the same and worse than the last one. The subject matter deals with drug stuff. And, uh, I don't think we cut any corners as far as profanity goes. And, uh, it deals with bad relationships and all that kinda crap.
Slash, August 1991

There's some stuff about what's gone on in our pasts, some stuff that's gone on in history that we all care about. Sex, things about Hollywood, different aspects of sex...
Duff, describing some of the lyrical topics, April 1990

LIFE ON THE ROAD

We were two years on the road.
When they finally dropped me off
at the airport I had no place to go.
Slash, 1992

Each individual in the band takes it differently. I'm a road guy, I'm into it, I don't like to go home, there's nothing to do there. For Axl, he's so conscious of himself and working on himself that being on the road for a long time can be sorta rough sometimes. But he does it, y'know? But like me, he wants everything to be the best it possibly can. And when you're falling apart in one way or another it's hard to keep up that level of integrity. Me, I love it, I'm on some weird jet-lag schedule, I never even know whether it's six in the morning or six at night.
Slash, May 1992

I sat in my hotel room all day today, looking at a pile of faxes and papers, a million things that need my attention. And I don't know, something just came over me. I took my Halliburton briefcase and smashed every light fixture in the room with it. Sometimes I don't know what's real anymore, and what isn't.
Axl, 1992

These days I just stay in my room, have a few drinks and play my stereo. It's so much less hassle. But there have been occasions when I fancied getting away from the security that surrounds us. I've been very clever, slipped quietly out of my room when no-one was around, got into the lift and was about to congratulate myself on getting away, when I'd spot one of the bodyguards waiting for me in reception with his arms folded! But you know,

I deal with it because being on the road is sort of normal for me. I've missed touring and everything that goes with it.
Slash, 1991

I do therapy as often as it can be. I've done 10 or 20 years of work in about a year and I can't stop. I've got to the point where I don't have a choice. I do the work or I go down the tubes. It's my destiny to be dealing with this crap. I have to do it to pull off this tour.
Axl, June 1992

Axl and Duff with Lemmy from Motörhead.

I have to take a security guy with me on the road now, cos they're scared I'm gonna die, or something.
Slash, June 1988

Izzy with Keith Richards.

It was the biggest thrill I ever had working with this band (The Rolling Stones), but it was also pretty nerve-wracking cos… we did four gigs in LA, right?… At six in the morning of the first one Axl called me, completely hammered, and told me, 'I'm quitting'. I told the other guys, 'It's gonna be a long four days, fellas'. Then he went onstage that night and announced he was quitting in front of 80,000 fucking people. How we managed to get through those gigs, I'll never know. There was so much shit raining down on us. Axl's mood to quit, the drug problems, the Steven problem, the whole 'One In A Million' controversy… plus I had a court date the morning after the last Stones date, at eight in the morning for pissing in a trash-can on an airplane, and I was facing six months in jail because I had a prior arrest for drug possession. So that was a fucking major psycho-time.
Izzy, October 1991

Out there on tour, you get hit by things when you're on stage, you jump into the crowd. It's like, no-holds-barred, relentless fucking rock'n'roll. To me that's what high-energy rock'n'roll is all about. I punch my guitar when we play and I come out of shows all bloody…
Slash, March 1989

I just think it's a really weird job. I'm not saying it's a bad job, I'm not saying it's a great job. But you know, it's just the work that goes into being that athletic. I mean, do you want to go out every night and jump off, like, your car? And have to do that? It's like it becomes your job. That doesn't take away the sincerity or the honesty of it, but it is a job. And sometimes I'd rather be doing something else.
Axl, April 1992

The band were realy brought down by the event (the 1988 Castle Donington show, where two fans died during the band's set). And we did try to stop the craziness down the front by changing our set, slowing things down. I actually don't know if the accident was our fault or not. If someone were to ask me face-to-face whether Guns n' Roses were to blame I couldn't say with any conviction that we're not. I don't think we can be held responsible, but I'd have to think very hard before giving an answer. Maybe we have to take some of the

Slash with Dave Mustaine of Megadeth.

blame. After all, we were onstage when those kids died, and had Guns n' Roses not existed then perhaps the tragedy wouldn't have occured. It weighs very heavily on us and whatever anyone else may write or say about the incident can't make us feel any worse. Quite honestly, we couldn't give a fuck about the media trying to make us the scapegoats. That thing will haunt me forever anyway.
Duff, June 1989

This tour, I just hope I don't die.
Axl, June 1992

I've been hotel-hopping for the last three to four years. Even when I'm home in town (LA), I stay in hotels.
Slash, May 1992

I'm a complete road dog.
Slash, July 1991

EX N' DRUGS N' BOOZE

Every night's a fucking party, man
Chicks, beer, you name it
Take any chick you want, man
It's like being in a candy store
Matt Sorum, October 199

We're a bad-boy band. We're not afraid to go to excess with substances, sexually and everything else. We know we're always going to be at odds with people on something. A lot of people are afraid to be that way. We're not. And the reason is that the bands who have made it real big are the ones who have been that way. And Guns n' Roses plan on making it real big.
Axl, June 1987

Sex is a lot better than getting into fights! I can remember my best sexual experiences way over how pissed off I've been. Good sex only comes every so often.
Slash, December 1988

I have a tendency to get really drunk and then I get to the hotel and I'll pick the first chick up that I can get. You'd be surprised at some of the chicks I've picked up.
Slash, June 1988

There's a time to do drugs and there's a time to drink and there's a time to do what you've got to do... And you've got to realise the difference.
Duff, September 1991

Rock musicians, like the guys in this band anyway, are all such fucking sensitive and volatile individuals. That's where the drug problems have come from.
Slash, 1992

There was that rape charge, which is basically old news... Three of us supposedly OD'd. We had been busted on drug charges in England and had been dropped from our label. I was supposedly this bisexual heroin addict who had AIDS and was into small animals. There's been a rumour a week about this band...
Axl, June 1987

It's strange, but tragedy and pain seem to dog our career. A lot of weird shit happens to this band. We seem to attract it. I dunno, I can't help wondering if the reason why Slash and Izzy were so strung out on 'certain substances' recently was their way of attempting to hide and numb the pain they felt.
Duff, June 1989

I just liked it (heroin). I liked the way it felt. And fuck, I didn't know if I did it four or five days in a row I'd get fucking hooked on it! And that's a different subject altogether. That drug takes you over mentally and physically, so much that to come back is hard. I was never a big coke addict, ever. I had not so much a drinking problem as to just want a drink and get rowdy. I used to love to get just fucking drunk! I used it to escape a bad day. Sometimes, I'd much rather just go home, sit down with a glass or something and kick back and go to sleep. I really don't feel that I have the intense addiction that people believe.
Slash, July 1991

Before and after the gig I'd have my dealer meet me. I'd built a place in the hotel room to hide my shit. Axl was tripping on the whole thing but as far as I was concerned I was fine - at least the gig was happening and I was playing.
Slash, February 1991

You know there are some people in this business who take drugs just cause they'd get fat if they drank. They should join us and go on The Jack Daniel's Plan!
Slash, June 1992

It (drinking) is a habit I picked up when I was 12 years old. It helps me, it brings me out of my shell. Because I cannot deal with people in a social situation when I'm sober. If I don't have a drink, I sink into myself. And I like it! I like being drunk, it's fun. I'm usually quite a good drinker, though I admit I can be a bit obnoxious when I'm drunk sometimes.
Slash, December 1988

I was forced into rehab once when I was going through a very big needle phase. Three days. And I saw what that was all about, and looked in the Yellow Pages and got a car and got myself out of there. I said, 'I'm not this fucked up!'
Slash, July 1991

People talk about how wrong it was doing drugs. Maybe they were the only tools I could find then...
Axl, 1992

I get hassled for, like, drinking Black Death. Influencing the youth of America. What?! I didn't know that was my gig!
Slash, May 1992

The afternoon we found out we would have to quit the (Iron) Maiden tour I went around grabbing every bottle of Jack I could find stashed around our dressing room and took it all back to the hotel. That was five days ago

and I've been living off it ever since. But now I'm down to my last bottle and a half. After that, I guess I'll be back to buying my own...
Slash, June 1988

When we get up in the afternoon to do a soundcheck we drink so much that we can't play, because our hands are shaking like windmills. So what happens? We drink! We drink more and more, and then we're fine, and we wake up the next day with some floosie... you don't know her name... you've got weird shit on your dick... your bed's all wet from pissing in it, and you go, 'Listen, will you do me a favour and find me some booze and some pizza?'
Slash, 1987

Drinking hurts my throat.
Axl, 1988

A bottle (of Jack Daniel's) a day for five years, that's what I was doing... you have really bad breath in the morning... you know, you can't have sex in the morning till you've brushed your teeth, which is a real fucking drag.
Slash, October 1988

We're all basically the same age... early 20s... and when you're that age, and you're in a band in Hollywood, and you're drinking a lot, and there are so many opportunities around, you go nuts!
Duff, May 1988

I moved into an apartment, the cheapest apartment I could find off Sunset Boulevard - that's how demented I am, right?... and we just used to party all the time... And I got so wrapped up in dope and coke and all the fucking scum that goes along with it that finally it just got out of hand. So I cleaned up and bought a house. Then I sat in the house for a while and hated it. I'd lay in bed and stare at the ceiling. There was nothing to do. And then I got back into it and got strung out in a serious way, where everybody was really worried, and I had some close run-ins with the police.
Slash, 1991

We've been through drugs and trying to figure out if you want to have one woman or you want to fuck everything that walks. I'm very much in love with a girl I've been with for the last two years. The first year was fine. I was home recording stuff. The next year I went back on the road and reverted to my bad old ways.
Slash, June 1992

I went out with a porno star for a while… I went to a party with the Metallica guys and got so drunk it got to the point where they were carrying me around, and I woke up the next morning in this chick's apartment. It was just after John Rawls, the porno star, died of AIDS. But I was like in hell, and she had a flat tyre and no phone. I was stranded with no money and it was just way fucked up. She used to do these things called lodes, which are the equivalent of heroin but they're pills. So she was out of it the whole time and impossible to talk to. My first question to her the next morning was, 'You haven't fucked good old John, have you?' I mean, no, she never fucked him. I found out so it was OK. But at first I was freaking…
Slash, June 1988

Rock'n'roll is, like, get loose, get laid and fucking go out and… well, y'know…
Slash, August 1991

…Even though I'm not shooting up or anything anymore, I'm still a nutcase when it comes to extracurricular activities.
Slash, 1992

Why do I drink? Why do I take drugs? Because it feels good. It's better than being bored and it helps me relax.
Slash, June 1992

Metal stems from sexual frustration. We come from an amazing background of repression, stifled childhoods…
Slash, June 1987

I didn't fuck a girl in a bar in New York like it said across a whole page in People magazine. My mom rang me that time. She said, 'You had your pants down in a bar on a Saturday night?' I said, 'No, hey, you know me. I'd have gone to the bathroom if I'd been going to do that'.
Slash, June 1992

A band can keep you together… but if you don't have a band, don't have a job, then somehow drugs seem to take over.
Slash, 1987

Let's face it, a lot of what we do stems from sexual repression in our childhood.
Slash, 1988

…I don't think he (David Bowie, an old flame of his mother's) was in any was responsible for my drug situation. I grew up around a lot of that kind of stuff so I knew what went down. I saw a lot of people go down. I saw a lot of heavy shit so I knew all about the downside, but I chose not to care for a long time. I knew what I was doing to myself but I didn't want to

stop. If anything I'd have to give credit to David Bowie the other way 'round... he helped me to get out of the heavy shit I was into. I met him about three years ago, it was the first time I'd seen him for years, and I told him about some bad hallucinations I'd been having. He said he'd been through the same sort of thing and we chatted about it. He didn't tell me to do anything in particular, but he did help me and he convinced me to change a lot of things with my life.
Slash, June 1992

Luckily I went through different shades of that (drug-taking) when I was really young, so I had the chance not to be some bitter 35-year-old still dealing with drug problems cos I thought I was having a good time earlier. I managed to get through it and see it. I've been clean now from heroin and all that for three years. I didn't wanna turn around and go through it again. I've learned that I can't sit, I can't have idle time, it doesn't suit me. Womanising is another thing; I just sort of grew out of that too. Most people, they're musicians but at the same time there's a lure to draw them into it... as many chicks as you want and as much dope as you want... I didn't come from that school.
Slash, May 1992

The only thing that bothered me was the drug thing. I've dabbled in it and everything, but nothing like what you hear that they do! When I went into it I thought I'd be walking into an opium den!
Matt Sorum, September 1991, referring to his recruitment

...That cocaine is obnoxious, and you can't get it up! And you get into these really ridiculous bitter fights. And then when you do a lot of coke, you tend to drink a lot...
Slash, July 1991

I drink a bottle of Jack Daniel's a day. Am I gonna die?
Slash, 1988

I was a major heroin addict. Got to the point where I was shooting anything up. Finally I got into trouble in a hotel and I nearly went to prison. That's when I took a plane out and kicked.
Slash, June 1992

I went into rehab once when I was going through a big needle phase. I lasted three days, that's all. I just hired a car and got the fuck out of there. I knew I wasn't fucked up enough to be in rehab so I just got away from the whole scene for a while. I was lucky to be able to do that but I don't think I was ever in as bad shape as some people thought.
Slash, June 1992

Of course I took ten grams of coke with me (to rehab). I'd be telling the limo driver to stop at a restaurant to get me a silverware set and he'd come back with a knife and a fork. I'd be like, 'No, the complete set...'
Slash, February 1991

I really should be dead by now. That's how bad it was. I guess I always felt indestructable. And that if I died, I didn't care about that either. I'd OD'd lots of times, would wake up and go, 'What happened?'
Slash, February 1991

If drinking doesn't get me, AIDS will.
Slash, June 1988

...Well, obviously I don't wanna be alive and have holes in my dick, d'you know what I mean?
Slash, August 1991

We always had a problem when we played here (San Francisco) before, cos we'd try to cop this China White heroin and end up paying ungodly prices for fucking nothing!
Izzy, October 1991

...If I'm not busy and focussed, I get loaded to pass the time.
Slash, July 1991

If you were to ask, as a therapist, 'Why do I drink?'... the simple thing is you do it out of

boredom and to relax. The worst thing is it's for people who are so volatile and so shy... you end up drinking a lot to come out of your shell. In that way it's a vicious sort of drug, because it works.
Slash, July 1991

You just gotta keep the shit in check. I've been drinking a lot for a long time and I'm only 23-years-old, and I know that, right? It's not something that I'm just so ignorant about that I'm going on this major blow out, until all of a sudden something stops me physically. I'm more aware than that, but I'll do it anyway. So if anything does happen, I won't be complaining about it, cos I knew, you know?
Slash, October 1988

I don't know how long my system will hold up. I could be superhuman and drink forever, you know what I mean? We are a young band and we've got a real hunger for… everything. And that will last as long as it lasts. I know anybody who thinks they're gonna be king of the hill forever has got it wrong. See, I learned that, cos of my background with my parents and shit. I've seen everything. I've seen the worst. And I've never met a person who hasn't quit while they're ahead, or it's fucked up their lives. The thing about coke and dope and Valium and shit like that, you have a great time and it's the best, but eventually it catches up with you. And if it catches up with you and you don't take notice and you get real arrogant about it, it'll… you'll be sitting in a rehab centre or going to AA meetings every fucking day. It's just not worth it to go through all that shit.
Slash, June 1988

I was in this golf resort hotel and I just wrecked the fucking place. I thought these two little guys were after me and they had these huge fucking knives. I ran outside through this golf resort and I just broke everything. I couldn't believe the damage I'd done when I saw it the next day. And I hurt myself pretty bad too. I was naked when I ran out and I cut my arms, my legs, my face, everywhere. I don't want to go into what I was on at the time, it was a combination. But that really forced me to quit a lot of the weird shit I was doing. You don't need it.
Slash, June 1992

I wrote some really cool shit when I was high.
Slash, July 1991

I don't do cocaine anymore. Well, only occasionally.
Slash, May 1992

…We all like to party, and party like hell, but we've a better idea now where the line is and we try not to go too far over it. We went to the precipice and we just opted to stay on the smart side of it… That's why we're still here.
Slash, June 1992

(Drugs) were doing me in. I felt like shit all the time. I went to somewhere where I knew I couldn't score, I had some Codeine with me and a few Valium to take the edge off, and I basically sweated it out. I made it through the 72-hour period but then I started drinking like a fish. I gave that up as well a couple of months later. I've been told that alcohol's no good for American-Indian blood which I've got in me. Alcohol really does fuck me up. It makes me crazy. I become impossible to deal with. I knew that I couldn't afford to fuck up any more. I'd used up all my 'Get Out Of Jail Free' cards.
Izzy, 1992

I did miss using drugs. I'd been used to living with them. But I'd gone through many problems in my life trying to stop, and when I started learning how to get along without them, I felt glad to be free of all that bullshit that went along with it - the scoring, the rip-offs, the bad drugs, the day-to-day hassle.
Izzy, 1992

WOMEN

We love to take care of women - we love to
treat them great... but right now we don't
have any money so we treat them like shit.

Izzy, 1986

All the guys had their girlfriends in the 'Sweet Child...' video, and I cut all my scenes out. There was one picture of my hand on her (his girlfriend's) ass and that was it. I'm not into drawing attention to the personal side.
Slash, May 1992

It took me all that time (two years) to create the situation and for my life to evolve to the point where it was proper for me to call her.
Axl, June 1992, referring to his relationship with model Stephanie Seymour

I can't handle having a girlfriend. I can get laid any time.
Slash, June 1988

I don't get horny when I write songs, and I'm not really that emotionally affected by women... I'm one of those people who's probably made himself hardened to falling in love...
Slash, December 1988

I've being doing a lot of work and found out I've had a lot of hatred for women. Basically, I've been rejected by my mother since I was a baby. She's picked my stepfather over me ever since he was around and watched me get beaten by him. She stood back most of the time. Unless it got bad, and then she'd come and hold you afterward. She wasn't there for me. My grandmother had a problem with men. I've gone back and done the work and found out I overheard my grandma going off men when I was four. And I've had problems with my own masculinity because of that. I was pissed off at my grandmother for her problem with men and how it made me feel about being a man.
Axl, April 1992

I was raised in a family where if a woman wore pants she was going to hell!
Axl, April 1992

I remember saying that I liked seeing two women together, and there were letters from lesbian organisations saying, 'How disgusting!' I can be as disgusting as the next person, but it wasn't meant to be disgusting. I think women are beautiful. I don't like to see people used. If I'm looking at a men's magazine and I look at the surface, I might be able to enjoy it. But if I know that this person is really messed up and that person's messed up and they're being used by the person who set up the photo session, then it'll turn my stomach.
Axl, April 1992

Sometimes there's these girls backstage going, 'I love you'. I feel like saying, 'Honey, if you knew me, you would hate my fucking guts'.
Axl, 1989

There's a lot to say for the period of time when you start to lose the excitement of chasing chicks. You start going after really bizarre girls, like librarians and stuff, just to catch 'em,

to say 'I finally went out and caught a girl that wouldn't be my normal date'.
Slash, 1987

Relationships with the opposite sex can be really fucked up now, because of the position we're in. Everybody's trying to get a piece of something.
Slash, May 1992

In LA it's real hard to find a wife.
Duff, 1992

I've been hell on the women in my life, and the women in my life have been hell on me. And it really breaks me down to tears a lot of times when I think about how terribly we've treated each other. Erin (Everly, the former Mrs. Rose) and I treated each other like shit. Sometimes we treated each other great, because the children in us were best friends. But then there were other times when we just fucked each other's lives completely up.
Axl, April 1992

Y'know, I detect a little bit of anti-feminism shit going on too (on 'Use Your Illusion'), because the songs that are about women that are really negative are like really fucking hard. I can see girls going, 'What assholes!' But then, y'know, our angle is just like, 'This is true you fucking cunt'. This is the way it was and we put it down on paper. But you know, these feminist groups will be like... d'you know what I'm saying?
Slash, August 1991

...It's hard for me to go and pick up chicks sometimes, cos I resent the fact that I'm getting laid cos I'm in a band.
Slash, June 1988

I don't leave my girlfriends lying around where my guitars are!
Slash, December 1988

I spend more money on women than I do on anything else!
Slash, June 1992

AXL

They (the fans) don't like it when
I let them know they don't own me.
Sometimes I don't even own myself!

Axl, April 1992

I wasn't told I had a real father until I was 17.
My real father was my stepdad, as far as I
knew. But I found some insurance papers, and
then I found my mom's diploma, with the last
name Rose. I was never born Bill Bailey. I was
born William Rose. I am W. Rose because
William was an asshole.
Axl, April 1992

I must say that Axl has fucking balls.
Duff, January 1990

Axl is not a person who wants to spend even
one second in a police station if he can avoid it.
Slash, June 1992

Yeah, I'm real spoiled. I've spoiled myself.
Axl, April 1992

I came with a nice big package of defects. So I
do past-life regression therapy work with a
homeopathic doctor.
Axl, June 1992

I said don't pick the mike-stand back up,
motherfucker!
**Axl to his roadie, onstage in San Francisco,
October 1991**

Hey, check it out... I'm having one of those
irrational temper tantrums you keep reading
about in the press.
Axl, as above, October 1991

Axl is just another version of the Ayatollah.
Slash, 1986

He's a bit eccentric, one of a kind. You've just
got to kind of go with it. We get along really
well. He's, you know, a different kind of cat.
Matt Sorum, September 1991

How the fuck did I get so fucking important?
Axl, 1992

Axl's so fucking great. Anything he does or says,
it's just because that's the way he really is. He's
beyond real, you know. I've never seen anyone
dare to talk shit to him, ever. I love that.
Matt Sorum, 1991

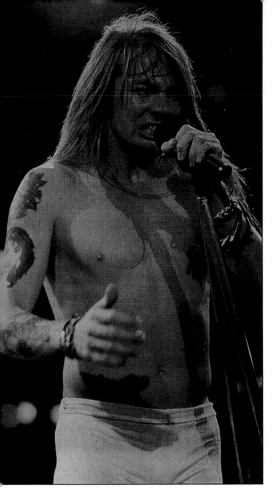

wait… it drives me nuts. That hour-and-a-half or two-hour time period that I'm late onstage is living hell, because I'm wishing there was any way on earth I could get out of where I am and knowing I'm not going to be able to make it. I'm late to everything. I've always wanted to have it written in my will that when I die, the coffin shows up a half-hour late and says on the side, like in gold, 'SORRY I'M LATE'.
Axl, April 1992

Every day there was a different story on the radio in the US about Axl dying. There was even one report that I'd shot him!
Slash, 1988

In the press Axl gets all this shit which I feel sorry for him about. Sometimes he asks for it, but a lot of the time he doesn't… there are times when I can't believe the shit he does, and a lot of the time he can't believe the shit that Slash or myself do, or Izzy does.
Duff, September 1991

I've been accused of thinking my shit doesn't stink. And it does, and maybe sometimes it stinks a lot worse than other people's.
Axl, April 1992

Axl might seem like a pain in the ass to everybody involved, but at the same time he's as dedicated to it as I am… even more so in many ways.
Slash, 1992

I sing in about five or six different voices that are all part of me, it's not contrived…
Axl, June 1987

Axl isn't really 24, he's a million years old… he's seen everything.
Izzy, 1986

Well, as you can see, being a fucking psycho basket-case like me does have it's advantages.
Axl, October 1991

I pretty much follow my own internal clock, and I perform better later at night. Nothing seems to work out for me until later at night. And it is our show. I don't want to make people sit around and

The way I've been attacked has been strange. The press has actually helped me get my head more together.
Axl, 1992

Axl's just naturally late. It can get pretty tense at times, particularly when you're supposed to be onstage and you're sitting there, literally counting the seconds, thing 'Man, we've just had a riot in St. Louis. Now we're in Texas. What the fuck is gonna happen here?'
Izzy, October 1991

Axl, lyrically, is brilliant in my eyes. Some of the shit that goes through his head is like, WHOA!
Duff, September 1991

Some people say I got a chip on my shoulder.
Axl, 1987

Homophobic? I think I've got a problem, if my dad fucked me in the ass when I was two. I think I've got a problem about it.
Axl, April 1992

In a lot of ways he (Axl's) the most normal guy in the band.
Duff, 1991

Axl wants to do stuff his way, at his pace, in his time.
Izzy, October 1991

If Axl was the nicest, quietest guy in the world he'd never sell any records.
Gilby Clarke, 1992

He ain't EVER going to lose this anger!
Duff, May 1988

My growth stopped at two years old. And when they talk about Axl Rose being a screaming two-year-old, they're right.
Axl, April 1992

Some of Axl's lyrics are fucking hilarious!
Slash, March 1989

I'm around a three-year-old baby now and then, and sometimes after a few days it's just too overwhelming for me. My head is spinning because of the changes it's putting me through.
Axl, April 1992

Before he used to be one of those guys who, if he thought someone was looking at him weird, would just haul off and smack 'em. And sometimes, y'know, the people he went for weren't even looking at him.
Izzy, October 1991

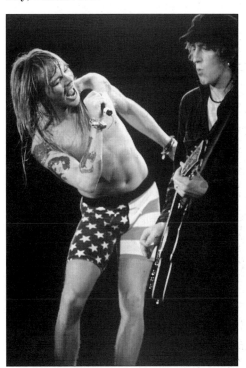

Generally, if I'm late I'm suicidal...
Axl, June 1992

Me an' Axl are so unalike that we attract each other.
Slash, July 1991

The relationship between most lead singers and most lead guitar players is very sensitive, very volatile. It's just very, very intense. It has major ups and major downs, there's always big mood swings and arguments. Singers and lead guitar players are very temperamental, everyone wants to have their own way. To be a lead guitar player or a singer you have to

have a real big ego! But somewhere within all this intensity and this friction, there's a chemistry. And if the chemistry is right, as with Axl and me, then there's something... a spark, or a need... that holds it together. But you fight too...
Slash, December 1988

The biggest fights are between me and Axl. But that's also what makes it happen.
Slash, July 1991

Okay, there were some security guys - we're talking about front-line house people, right? And the guys are fucking standing there with

Axl with Mick Jagger.

their arms on the stage watching the band, okay? And there was this gang of guys, and they're taking pictures and shit. And Axl says to the security, 'Are you gonna do anything about it?' And then he says, 'Well, if you're not, I will!' That's Axl, bam, right in there. And we kept the suspense beat going, but when he got back onstage it was just like, 'Fuck this' and he threw his mike down. That's just the way he is, alright?
Slash, August 1991, referring to the infamous St. Louis riot

I went to a clinic thinking it would help my moods. The only thing I did was take one 500-

question test... you know, filling these little black dots. And all of a sudden I'm diagnosed manic depressive! Let's put Axl on medication... Except the medication didn't work. The only thing it does is help keep people off my back cos they figure I'm on medication.
Axl, 1989

I guess I like who I am now. I'd like to have a little more internal peace. I'm sure everybody would.
Axl, April 1992

SLASH

I didn't have any big dreams about being
a womanising drug addict alcoholic.

Slash, May 1992

My mom and dad were both in the music business very major. We used to be, like, really rich, as far as that goes. Growing up in Stoke-On-Trent was great, an entirely different atmosphere, a different set of morals as far as things considered important. In Northern England there's a difference in what's held in high regard. It's a lot tougher, school is different. I fought a lot when I was young; I'm usually calm now. We moved to Laurel Canyon in '77 when I was 12 and that was the beginning of my slippery slope. The public school system in the US really sucks. There was nothing to hold my attention so I just fucked off. And then I started playing guitar… that was the beginning of the end.
Slash, June 1992

It wasn't because I had a problem with the bathroom, it wasn't a bladder thing.
Slash, May 1992, explaining the acquisition of his name

When I was in England I was very strange because I was the only kid with long hair. When I came to LA and started school I never really fitted in. I didn't really have a group of friends. Then what happened when I was 13 years old, I just thought 'Fuck it' and didn't worry about it any more; then all of a sudden everyone was cool, and I started becoming popular.
Slash, December 1988

… I don't like being stared at or being the stereo-typical Slash.
Slash, 1991

No, but I try to!
Slash, May 1992, when asked if he got a blow-job every day

I didn't really know how to start; I was looking at a book playing scales and didn't know where I was going, cos that didn't sound anything like 'Cat Scratch Fever', you know? But my grandmother used to play piano, and she got me my first guitar. She was very patient and supportive, especially because she'd come from a rich black family where, at the time, soul music was considered in bad

taste and she wasn't even allowed to listen to it. So when I'd crank up 'Black Dog' she'd get really upset… she'd been raised to hate stuff like that. And of course, being the punk that I was, I'd crank it up even higher.
Slash, February 1991

I've been voted 'Best Guitarist' in the polls conducted by a number of magazines across the world. But this doesn't mean I'm the best in the world. It's simply that my band is really popular.
Slash, 1989

…It's not so much how good a player you are, it's how cool you are.
Slash, March 1989

My favourite cartoon characters are Metallica and Slash.
Axl, 1989

My playing is my priority…
Slash, July 1991

I don't think it (his guitar) is a phallic symbol. I don't think it is a symbol of anything. Basically, as far as what I use a guitar for it's just something to hide behind, because I'm quite shy.
Slash, December 1988

I've got my fucking bag full of clothes and that's everything, right? And I've got my cooler. I've got my booze in there and that's all I fucking need.
Slash, August 1991

table when the police come to call; nodding out on the table at restaurants - shit like that. I love the guy a lot, but the fact is, man, Slash is not what you'd call the thinking man's drug user. He's really careless, doing really shitty things like OD-ing in other people's apartments.
Izzy, October 1991

In a world he did not create, he will go through it as if it were his own making; half-man, half-beast, I don't know what it is, but it's weird and it's pissed off and it calls itself Slash!
Axl, 1989

When I was a kid I always had animals around. And I always had this thing for snakes. I used to go to the Renaissance Faire every day here and catch frogs, lizards, snakes... I'd put them all in a huge tank. The lizards would eat the snake eggs, the snake would eat the frogs, or whatever. It was really fascinating. I got to learn about the whole cycle of life.

I have had a couple of poisonous snakes in

I just couldn't live any other way though. I'd be bored out of my mind. I don't care what kind of toll it takes on me in the long run. I'd rather live fast now than live slow and die with white hair and having never done anything I ever wanted to do.
Slash, June 1992

To me, my whole philosophy is, like, go out there and fucking rage.
Slash, October 1988

I haven't even voted. There's no-one to vote for. For me it's like, 'Fuck, does my amp work?'
Slash, May 1992

I've always been sort of a night person.
Slash, February 1991

... Well, let's just say that he can pronounce his syllables better now. He was pretty bad though. Fuck, he was a mess. He's a great guy an' all, but he can't monitor his own intake, with the result that he's always fucking up big-time. Like leaving dope hanging out on the

my time, but one of the rattlers got out once and scared the whole family. I had visions of one of those B horror movies! And one time me and Izzy caught a five-foot Pacific rattler, without any tools... that was a real experience. I wanted to take him home, but at the time I was living in the same room with Axl and two anacondas... so I let him go.
Slash, February 1991

Oh, I have snakes and cats and dogs and an alligator and tiger lizards and all kinds of stuff. That's why I don't go home. It's busy in there. There's too much going on. I've got dinosaurs all over the place, too. Not real ones. I couldn't find one. Apparently, no one has been able to for some years.
Slash, May 1992

If I was going to die, it would have to be because the stage collapsed or a lighting truss fell on me or something. I'd hate to go out because of self-pity.
Slash, July 1991

I'm not nervous onstage. I get into being up there; it's this huge energy release. When I'm up onstage, that's my element. But, at the same time, I have a lot of hair over my face and really avoid eye-contact, I've also got my guitar to hide behind and I'm completely in my own world up there. I couldn't be a lead singer, there's no way I could do that.
Slash, December 1988

I was certainly going through my problems at the time (of the Rolling Stones shows at the LA Coliseum, 1989) and trying to come to terms with the whole situation, which wasn't easy. So that colours my perspective on those gigs with the Stones. And I never met any of the band, which was deliberate. Somehow there were so many people setting us against the Stones - you know, the bad boys of rock'n'roll come face to face... that I wasn't interested in hanging out with Keith Richards and seeing which one of us would end up drinking the most Jack Daniel's. I love the Stones, but it was the wrong situation to meet them. They had such an enormous entourage hanging round with them that it all seemed so divorced from

what I'm about. Other guys in the band met them and had their photos taken, but it wasn't for me.
Slash, 1990

About a year and a half ago Slash got pulled over in LA for drunk-driving and this was when he was using heroin a lot, right? Anyway, I was staying at a hotel in Venice and he showed up at four in the morning, fucked out of his mind. How he managed to drive

there will always a mystery to me! So I let him spend the night. The next morning I find two rigs (syringes) hidden in the closet. I told him, 'Listen fucker, I got problems and I just can't have this shit around', cos I was on probation for six months at the time.
Izzy, October 1991

Most guitarists start playing guitar to get them laid, to look cool or to get some heavy image. I started playing guitar out of ignorance, because I wanted to play an instrument that was rock'n'roll orientated, but I didn't know

back then the difference between bass and lead guitar or any of that shit! I basically chose the guitar because it had more strings.
Slash, December 1988

When we hired the (private) plane, Slash was having trouble justifying our spending that much money. I said, 'But dude, you're a rock'n'roll star!' He looked at me and said, 'You almost made me throw up!'
Axl, June 1992

I was given a lot of freedom as a kid. I grew up in a kind of rebellious hippy household. I started saying the word 'fuck' when I was, like, seven or eight years old, telling my parents to 'fuck off' all the time. They were always very attentive and I don't have any problems with

Slash with Brian May (centre) and with Sebastian Bach of Skid Row (below).

know how to use one if I did. And I'm really not a violent guy at all. I just felt something had to be said. Sometimes you gotta draw the line for people.
Slash, June 1988

It's like, I don't have any serious concern in the back of my head about how long I'll live or how old I'll be as far as getting to be 60 or

my family, nothing at all compared to a lot of musicians who complain about getting kicked out of the house because they grew their hair, or were told to 'Fuck off and get a job!' I never had that. There was music in my house all my life.
Slash, December 1988

Listen, I'm not saying I was the first rock'n'roller to wear a top hat onstage. But look, man, CC (DeVille, Poison guitarist) is the type of guy who probably didn't even know what a top hat was until he saw me wearing one. You know, I caught up with him one night in the Rainbow, and I told him quietly, 'If I ever see you wearing a top hat onstage again I'm gonna shoot you...' I tell ya, he freaked, man! And I mean, I don't own a gun... wouldn't

I'm not one of those people who thinks guitars have tits and ass.
Slash, December 1988

I look back sometimes at the things I've done, and I see that what gets me off is working real hard towards something, to reach a goal.
Slash, February 1991

Know what I want to do? Really want to do? Go over to Japan and pollute it. I'm not talking about drugs, I'm talking about teenage sex, bring over some crazy porn magazines and drop them from the tops of tall buildings. There's no beaver shots in Japan...
Slash, June 1987

As far as being reincarnated, it doesn't weigh heavy on my mind, okay?
Slash, August 1991

something. But then I think that's the biggest cliche in the world from any fucking rock... uh... personality.
Slash, August 1991

A little perspective doesn't hurt. I just turned 25 and something went off in my head. When I started this I was 19, and at that there's nothing to stop you, so far as you can see. And then you get older - not to say I'm old now - but you change a little and see things differently. It's pretty natural.
Slash, February 1991

It's great. I'm 25 and I've met everybody!
Slash, July 1991

I don't judge people. For me, I'd probably do the same things if I wasn't in a band, if I was an accountant. I know what motivates me. I happen to love this whole thing. I wouldn't trade it for anything.
Slash, May 1992

Personally, I don't want to piss off anyone.
Slash, February 1991

I couldn't give a shit really.
Slash, June 1992

IZZY

If people think I don't respect Izzy
or acknowledge his talent, they're
sadly mistaken. He was my friend.

Axl, April 1992

Izzy sits in the corner and plays his guitar. He's very sarcastic.
Slash, 1989

The interviewer asks (Mötley Crüe's Vince Neil) about him throwing a punch at Izzy backstage at the MTV awards last year. Vince replies, 'I just punched that dick and broke his fucking nose! Anybody who beats up on a woman deserves to have the shit kicked out of them. Izzy hit my wife a year before I hit him...' Well, that's just a crock of shit. Izzy never touched that chick. If anybody tried to

and carried him along, onstage and all the rest of it, and it was OK. Then it got to the point where he didn't even show for the 'Don't Cry' video and we decided that this was getting ridiculous, it wasn't fair to anybody that he wasn't putting the same amount of input as everybody else. It came down to the wire and what happened happened.

We were sorta relieved. It's a little heavier now cos he sorta wishes he was still doing it, and we're sorta like... over it! Izzy hasn't been an issue.
Slash, June 1992

hit on anything, it was her trying to hit on Izzy when Vince wasn't around. Only Izzy didn't buy it. So that's what that's all about...
Axl, January 1990

Izzy's been keeping himself more or less clean for quite a while now, and the chaos of being on the road, especially with the rest of us driving him crazy, he just couldn't deal with. He's been 110% sober for the past two years...
Slash, 1992

Izzy just stopped wanting to do anything, so after a while it got to the point where... Put it this way, at first we were just like 'whatever'

There were responsibilities that Izzy didn't want to deal with. He didn't want to work at the standards that Slash and I set for ourselves. He just didn't want to do videos. He just wasn't into it. Getting Izzy to work on his own songs on this record was like pulling teeth.
Axl, April 1992

I've been straight for a year and a half now. No booze, no weed, nothing. I just stopped cold. I said, 'Fuck, I should give this a shot'. When I finally stopped and then started going out, just riding around on a fucking bicycle, I thought 'Wow, this is really cool. How did I forget all this simple shit?'
Izzy, October 1991

Izzy doesn't dig it all anymore. He don't dig the drinking, even.
Matt Sorum, October 1991

We got this letter saying, 'This changes, this changes, and maybe I'll tour in January'. And they were ridiculous demands that weren't going to be met. I talked to Izzy for four-and-a-half hours on the phone. At some points I was crying, and I was begging, I was doing everything I could to keep him in the band. There were stipulations, though; if he was going to do like the old Izzy did, he wasn't going to make as much money.

...When the guy's getting up at 6.30 in the morning and riding bicycles and motorcycles and buying toy airplanes, and he's donating all this energy into something else, and it's taking 100% of our energy to do what we're doing onstage, we were getting ripped off.

...I'm hoping Izzy's new album rocks. But at the same time it'll be like, 'Why couldn't he do that with us?' He wouldn't do anything. I'm angry with him because he left in a very shitty way, and he tries to act like everything's cool.
Axl, April 1992

Izzy on why he left the band

I knew deep inside that it didn't feel right. I didn't understand any more what was happening or what direction it was taking.

I had no idea when the record ('Use Your Illusion') was going to be finished. It was such a day-to-day existence, I never really knew what was happening. I didn't want to make promises unless I planned on keeping them.

I couldn't get the other guys to learn any cover songs with me or practice anything to fill in the space (when Axl wasn't on stage). I tried talking to Axl about it and he would just get pissed off. I was really fed up and unhappy with it. I felt there was nothing I could do to fix this thing.

It got to the point where the only thing you'd hear or read about was the antics. There was no talk of the music, which is what it is all meant to be about. If the band is constantly in the papers for things other than the music, it's weird.

We had a lot of drugs problems in the band from day one, but somehow we managed to rise above that with our music and records. With the 'Illusion' albums it kinda felt like the music had submerged beneath the bullshit.

I rarely saw the guy (Axl) except at gigs. The band had a great big aeroplane and I only rode it once I think.

The one thing I wanted to see was the gigs running on time. And whoever was responsible for being late should have been prepared to pay the late charges to the union guys. It's ugly that it comes down to money, but we fucked away hundreds of thousands of dollars over these late gigs. Then there was

the St Louis riot. We lost the PA, and that cost us a quarter of a million dollars. I didn't think it was fair for the band to keep turning up late. People have got jobs to go back to in the morning, they have families and kids, they've got to get babysitters, and I just figured, 'Shit, these people are shelling out money for tickets, and we should be on time. If the monitors are fucked, too fucking bad. We should just roll with it and try to get them working.

It was made clear to me how things were going to to be run (in Guns N' Roses). I slept on it and when I woke up in the morning, I said, 'That's the end of the line for me'. I just felt like my opinions were no longer considered valid. It wasn't about being a rock'n'roll band and playing music any more. Life is tough enough to live day to day without an extra 50lb of aggravation on your head.

The differences of opinion were between me and Axl. I tried to resolve the problems with him before I left, but it didn't look to promising. I'd known him for long enough to know what he was going to do things his own way, and I'd end up doing things my own way. We were both hard-headed in that sense.

I wouldn't say we (Axl and I) were big friends these days, but I've known him for too long to carry on grudges or resentment. I feel about having been in that band and done some of that music and some of those tours, and I don't have any permanent scars. I'm still able to keep my balance on a skateboard.

DRUMMERS

Steven... he's always been the child
of the band, the one that was always
just the happy-go-lucky, sex, drugs
and rock'n'roll and that's it.
Slash, July 1991

He (Steven Adler) needs peace of mind, cos
when he was young he had to go to the
hospital and they took a piece of it!
Axl, 1986

I hated Steven, he was a real little asshole. He
had a double-drum, all these drums and shit,
and he was just a little asshole. I love him now
to death, but he'll tell you himself, he was an
asshole then.
Duff, January 1990

was in a hospital trying to clean himself up. I
gave him every possible encouragement and
help. We all did. But there came a point when
if we had continued to wait for him then the
band itself might have been in serious trouble
and it could have split us up.
Slash, 1990

Firing Steven was so hard, I kept postponing
the decision even though I knew for a while
that it was gonna have to come. And when we
finally did the deed it was a Godsend.
Slash, 1991

I never wanted 'Steven Adler's on vacation', I
wanted 'Steven Adler's in a fucking rehab'.
Axl, April 1992

I personally went to his drug dealer with my
gun, went to his house and all this shit. We did
everything we could.
Duff, September 1991

A lot of rumours have been going around
suggesting that we abandoned him (Steven
Adler) because he had a drug problem. That's
not the case at all. We all had drug problems.
Yet we all came came through ours. And we
sat around for a year waiting for Steven to sort
himself out. I personally spent hours on the
phone with him and also visiting him when he

Once rehearsals began for the new record his
(Steven Adler's) chops were all over the place.
And he was lying to us on a daily basis. I was
trying to talk some sense into him but it never
happened. He wouldn't listen to anybody...
And Axl and Duff had had it.
   As amazing as it seems in this drug-free,
exercize and health age, there's a bunch of us

who are still clinging fast to the late '60s and '70s. But Steve never grew up to the fact that it's not all just sex, drugs and rock'n'roll. To him it was a big fantasy and we took care of him. And now he's on his own.

I did keep in touch. I'd pop into his house every now and then to see how he was doing. I stuck with him, as you'd do for a loved one. And then he started getting on my case, saying, 'I've heard you guys are on heroin and what's the difference, blah, blah, blah…' And finally, I couldn't talk to him any more. I'd take him out to dinner and it would turn into this huge fight, to the point where I couldn't take it.

So now I don't see him any more. I call his doctor and I think about him a lot. And I worry. Cos it's a scarey thing. And he was my best friend for a long time.
Slash, February 1991

Steven (Adler) is scared to death of me. If he sees me in public he just turns into a grovelling heap of defeatism.
Slash, 1992

Matt (Sorum) really did pull the band back together. He learned 38 tunes in a month, got them all down perfect.
Duff, 1991

He (Matt) was the kick in the ass that re-motivated us, because at one point I think we forgot what we were here for.
Slash, July 1991

One night when I was bummed Matt (Sorum) came around and put his hand on me: 'It's alright, man'. Those little things are really special.
Axl, April 1992

Me, I like to party. I'm like your typical drummer, I guess. Sometimes I go overboard.
Matt Sorum, October 1991

I just try to slam the drums as hard as possible and make the band crunch, as heavy as possible.
Matt Sorum, September 1991

THE BAND

KEEP
OUT
KNOCK FIRST
OR.
DIE

This band is what it is. It ain't no bullshit
It isn't sitting around thinking up ideas for
publicity. This stuff really happens! They're
just being themselves. So this is it, take it or
leave it, love it or hate it, that's why it works

Matt Sorum, September 199

I don't understand why people get so worked up about Guns n' Roses...
Slash, 1990

In the '60s it was The Rolling Stones, in the '70s it was Aerosmith and in the '80s it's Guns n' Roses.
Slash, 1988

We are the fucking band of the '90s!
Axl, June 1992

...The only real rock'n'roll band to come out of LA in the last ten years.
Axl, June 1987

I guess you could say we're turning into what you'd call a big band.
Slash, June 1988

We brought back that whole element of danger, along with a few other bands, which was severely lacking.
Slash, February 1991

Kids need a band like us.
Duff, January 1990

We're not like God or anything...
Duff, April 1990

We were rebels. We are rebels, and there weren't any rebels around in the early '80s. Fuck, even Punk got to be a fashion, and then it was dead. So the whole element of rock, that whole attitude, disappeared. We brought it back in a way. Kids got into it. All the way from the little kids who don't wanna take a bath at night to teenagers who are generally fucked up anyway, right through people who relate to this shit from their youth.
Slash, April 1990

Look, I don't know how influential people think we're supposed to be. I mean, like, we're an example now because we're a big band? No. Nononono.
Slash, August 1991

I know and understand that we have a lot of influence. But that's not where out attitude is. When we're out onstage we will say things about certain situations which arise, such as bottles being thrown. Apart from that we have never told people what to do with their lives. We've never advocated any kind of direction people who listen to our music should follow. I find it vaguely ridiculous what people expect from a rock band. But then, isn't it also true that all the attention any successful band gets is ridiculous?
Slash, September 1991

I don't know any more what people expect from us. They seem to be waiting to see what we'll do next. I feel as if I'm walking around in a circus act all day.
Slash, September 1991

You couldn't really hate us, because the band's real. Regardless of whether you like us or not, we're going to go on and still do what we do... We want to travel, continue the big Guns n' Roses adventure, and indulge ourselves. And fuck a lot!
Slash, June 1987

It's the music that's the bottom line with this band. We're not the easiest band in the world to work with, and we've basically got this 'screw you' attitude that gives a lot of people cause to worry. But we do know our limits. We

never segregated the audience in our minds as white, black or green.
Slash, March 1989

They still try and label us as a Glam band, but I don't give a shit because we're not.
Slash, June 1987

We don't want to associate ourselves with Glam, and the main reason is because that's what Poison associates themselves with. I've told those guys personally they can lock me in a room with all of them and I'll be the only one who walks out! They used to come to our shows before they ever played a gig. Everybody copying them? Sorry I don't see it. Poison came out in an article saying they started Glam... I don't know where they were in the '70s. The only reason I put my hair up is because Izzy had these pictures of Hanoi Rocks and they were cool, and because we hung out with this guy who studied Vogue magazine hairstyles and was really into doing my hair...
Axl, June 1987

We're not a business.
Duff, September 1991

stop if we think what we're doing is going to screw up our music.
Axl, June 1987

We're in a no-win situation; damned if we do, damned if we don't.
Slash, 1991

Maybe it would've been best for the purists if we'd died or broken up.
Axl, 1992

The band as a unit is stronger, because we've been through so much...
Slash, May 1992

We're not gonna change the world...
Slash, August 1991

One of the nice things about Guns n' Roses is that we've always been a people's band. We've

Poison.

This is the most highly organized unorganized bunch of people in the whole world.
Axl, January 1991

We are for real. We are not Glam shit or anything else. We are just Guns n' Roses.
Slash, 1989

I think one of the reasons people think we're cool is because we say things that people wouldn't dare to mention in regular life.
Slash, 1992

We'll probably always be controversial.
Slash, February 1991

We love each other. The whole band... we're like, real tight... I couldn't continue this band minus one of these guys.
Slash, June 1988

There's always a lot of tension going down between us. There's always something happening, sparks flying.
Slash, 1988

It is dangerous, it is threatening, and if anybody calls us out on anything we won't back down. This is what we mean. If you want to fuck with it, I don't care if I get killed or you kill me, because I believe in what I want. I believe in what we deliver.
Duff, 1991

We went so against the stream it was like wearing flippers in the sand.
Slash, April 1990

It's important for this band to do what it wants to and to keep close to our roots. We never have any intention of turning into a money-making machine, like other bands I could mention.
Slash, October 1991

...Really, the only family we have is the one between us. These guys, they're my sense of reality, they're the people I cling to...
Slash, May 1992

It's a brotherhood.
Duff, July 1991

That (Steven Adler's sacking) will be the last line-up change we make. The current band is it. I wouldn't want to see anyone else go.
Slash, shortly before Izzy's departure, October 1991

When we're not playing we're at a bar or some-where. We're on such a short fuse it's tough to say what we're going to be doing at any moment.
Slash, 1988

We're not conventional. Trust me, we're far, far, far away from being conventional.
Slash, April 1990

We may be fuck-offs in life but we're not fuck-offs in the studio.
Slash, September 1991

We never set out to be role models for kids. We're just us. If some kid is dumb enough to try to act like us, we take no responsibility for what might happen. The kind of life we lead is good for us... but we've been lucky. You could end up dead just as easily as having a number one album.
Slash, June 1992

We're the kind of band we liked when we were kids, definitely a people's band.
Slash, 1987

There's so much more significant things going on in the world than us. It's reality.
Slash, April 1990

We may just be a rock'n'roll band that doesn't know what it's fucking doing sometimes, but at least we're honest.
Duff, January 1990

There's no way of getting this band in any kind of regimented routine.
Slash, October 1991

There's only one photograph of the six of us in existence, can you believe that? Getting all the members of Guns n' Roses in the same room at the same time is very difficult.
Matt Sorum, October 1991

We're not really that sleazy, we just look that way when people compare us to a lot of other bands. If you compare us to a bunch of posers like some of the bands in LA, then we come across real 'street' and real sleazy.
Slash, 1988

We're not creating a hype. I can't figure us out, so why analyse it?
Slash, April 1990

We're very emotional.
Slash, May 1992

With the new band and the new people, it's the first time I've really felt at home. It used to be just the five of us against the world. Now we've brought some of the outside world into the

band. The first night we played with the new band, I was sitting at the piano during 'November Rain' just looking at this, and feeling really glad that I was a part of this thing.
Axl, 1992

We're not so much the punk band as we were, only because we've been doing it for a while and we're all sort of aspiring musicians...
Slash, July 1991

It all gets down to the fact that we are a rock'n'roll band who tells the truth in our songs, truths which would be recognised by anyone who, like us, comes from the wrong side of the tracks.
Duff, September 1991

Guns n' Roses as a band are really sincere. We may not be the best musicians in the world, and there are tighter bands and better stage shows. But when we're up there

We have pieces of everything in our band, and we try and find a way to bring it all out rather than limit our selves into one frame. You don't see a lot of that any more... Queen used to do it, and Zeppelin, but nowadays people tend to stay in one vein.
Axl, June 1987

We just fucking go out and when it's great it's great. When it sucks, fuck, we suck. That's the magic of it.
Slash, August 1991

we're fucking 120 percent into what we're doing.
Slash, December 1988

No matter who I play with outside of Guns n' Roses, my family is Guns. That's my priority and my whole life is based around that.
Slash, August 1991

My bond with this group is pretty much in my blood.
Slash, October 1991

To me it's only a rock band.
Slash, 1992

...In the whole scheme of things we're just a rock'n'roll band. Nothing more, nothing less. We're sitting here smoking cigs and having a drink, then we go home, fuck our girlfriends and go to bed. Then we wake up, go back to the studio to do another song or two. Fuck man, we've been asked to comment on things and stuff that are totally out of our league and we are apparently supposed to know everything about everything, just because we've sold a few million albums. Fuck, what do I know about Nelson Mandela being free?
Duff, April 1990

This band always has been, and always will be, volatile.
Duff, October 1991

We are not the Berlin Wall coming down. We are not Communism falling. We are not fucking civil war in Yugoslavia. We are not the Gulf war. We are just a fucking rock'n'roll band.
Duff, July 1991

We're not always gonna be the brash teenage hardcore band, because we won't always be brash and teenaged. Of course, kids hate hearing that, cos it reminds them that they're gonna get older someday too.
Slash, February 1991

FAME'N'FORTUNE

We were all sitting around with bits of paper trying to figure it out. Everyone came up with different numbers, but basically we stopped counting after we got past $100 million.
Axl, assessing the band's wealth, March 1990

Look, I really take all of this with a pinch of salt.
Duff, 1991

It was success that screwed us up.
Slash, 1992

It's pathetic... the less we do, the bigger the band gets. It's weird, because we haven't really done anything and we're real recognisable.
Slash, July 1991

It's been such a trip from having no money and notoriety to having all this money, notoriety, all these drug connections and bullshit.
Izzy, October 1991

I cope with it by not coping with it. Period. I try to go through life pretending it's not really that real. It only really slaps you in the face when you're out in public where there's a lot of your so-called crowds and your so-called bands. Especially going to concerts and clubs. We haven't being doing that lately. That's pretty much where it's realistic. When you're at home you forget about it. You watch TV or fuck your girlfriend... like everybody else does.
Slash, April 1990

I have this vivid memory of sitting literally on the sidewalk in front of The Marquee and drinking a bottle of Jack and just hanging out with people and shit and now I can't do something like that. I'm not complaining because it's a small price to pay. But I miss the complete detachment from responsibilities that everybody has to deal with in everyday life. Y'know, financially and everything that goes with it as far as apartments and houses and cars and... y'know, all that shit.
Slash, August 1991

It's really weird having had such success. I go to shows and people come up to tell me how great we are. And I think to myself, 'We haven't done anything yet!' Look, all this band has done so far is put out one LP and a half-assed mini-album. I often wonder if we deserve what's happening to us. Still, we did tour forever and certainly paid our dues. Having struggled for ten years in so many bands, it's nice to be in a position now to earn money from making music.
Duff, June 1989

...By the time the tour was over we were told we were mega... Spinal Tap, you know, 'You're great! You're great!' And we're still walking around trying to make sure you don't have a stain on your jeans after you take a piss kind of thing. And there's all this stuff going on around you, all these people treating you like you're on a pedestal even if you don't feel that way. So we went from nowhere to being this really huge band, not feeling any different, only having people tell you that and react to you a certain way.
Slash, July 1991

It's actually at the point where I go to a club and end up leaving totally depressed. It really brings me down. Everybody wants to have your undivided attention, and if you don't give it then they act like you're an asshole... turned into this big rock star, you know.
Slash, March 1989

The worst thing... is when you're off the road and you're trying to take a walk to a club, or you're out on the freeway, and then people recognise you and instantly screw your whole reality up because, all of a sudden, you're a Pop Star again. And I don't necessarily like being a Pop Star...
Slash, October 1991

I find that 'friends' of mine are trying to pick up on my girlfriend just cos I wasn't in town. Y'know? Really weird high school shit, kindergarten shit. And people making some sorta noise about what I do on the road, having a real ball. And I didn't realise we were that significiant. I can't walk around and it's a drag. My basic privacy is gone. I don't know, it's all so fucking complicated.
Slash, May 1992

Axl with Elton John at the Freddie Mercury Tribute.

We've had to adapt our lifestyles a little. If we go to clubs these days we have to expect to be hassled, and I've gotten into three fights recently with guys just trying to show off to their girlfriends. I won all of them though! You see, I've got a mountain bike that I constantly ride, so I'm in good shape.
Duff, June 1989

It's like, shall we act like Led Zeppelin and just go around with this huge entourage and not to talk to anybody so the mystique is happening and everybody's like 'Wow!'? No. We just wanna feel natural. I've been watching this develop. We have security and it's like, Bam! In the car! To the gig! So on and so forth. And, y'know, we don't wanna feel pompous. But people love to go, 'Oh yeah, the Guns guys. They're rock stars now. They're assholes'. None of us are like that. But how do you argue, y'know?
Slash, August 1991

You know, part of my difficulty is that I haven't changed at all, at least I don't think I have. Yet others seem to react differently to me now that Guns n' Roses has become so well-known. I walk into a 7-11 store and I have the feeling that people want me to walk on water or something. Or else I'll go into a bar and there'll be a guy who wants to get me a drink or else offers me some drugs. If I refuse, however politely, he'll call me a big-headed asshole. But if I take the bottle then I'm accused of being violent! You can't win, eh?
Slash, 1990

You can stay in the most expensive hotels and you can be a huge rock band and have a lot of fame and recognition and all that stuff, but when you get into the rooms, toilet paper is still toilet paper.
Slash, 1989

We can't walk down the street any more, or pop into a liquor store, without getting hassled. I guess it's the classic scenario, almost a cliche. I suppose every band's gone through it. And people who are just rock fans or people who would love to be in our shoes are sitting there going, 'Well, that's a small price to pay'... which to tell you the truth it is.
Slash, July 1991

We've adapted to it a little bit better than we had maybe a year ago when we started to get really big. Then it really screwed with us, now it's better.
Slash, 1991

It's not like it used to be. I used to be able to hang out at a bar all day and not be noticed. Now? Oh, I hang out at a bar all day and get hassled.
Slash, 1992

It's like walking around in Toonville, being a whole human being and walking around with all this shit going on around you. Ridiculous. But I'm used to it.
Slash, July 1991

Being famous is like living in Toonville, it's like being in a fucking cartoon. The only good thing about being famous is when you're onstage, everything else is just bullshit.
Slash, June 1992

I have a really hard time swallowing the concept of being any kind of rock fucking star.
Slash, August 1991

People recognise me really easily, but I don't think about it. I don't have the outgoing personality of, say, David Lee Roth. I used to be pretty social on the road, but it's more difficult now because we have security around us all the time... and when we do duck them we get into trouble! A few times I've ditched security and gone out on my own, but ended up with problems. There was one occasion when Duff and I went out by ourselves and got a couple of hotels rooms just to hang out. But I ended up in a huge fight with (comedian) Sam Kinison and Duff nearly got arrested for

punching him out!

If I go into a rock bar or a strip joint then I know that I'm going to get recognised and deal with it, because I wanna drink. But in restaurants or other places where you wouldn't expect recognition people still come out of the woodwork and get very pushy for autographs. But I never pull Rock Star Attitude trips and always oblige. Yet if you're trying to have a conversation with someone and you get a piece of paper shoved under your nose it can be a difficult situation. Sure, there is a lack of freedom, but I won't complain about it, because the only reason I'm here is the fact that I'm doing what I enjoy.
Slash, October 1991

known that security in my whole life, you know? Some people are like, 'Oh, why don't you give money to this or that you know, you have all this money...' I'm like, 'Well, no, I got a certain interest rate and I bought my security. You bought your house, didn't you? I worked for my livelihood too, you know?'
Axl, January 1990

We got offered $20 million to do one Marlboro cigarette print ad. We said 'Fuck you!' Firstly, the sell-out thing is bullshit. Secondly, maybe 25 percent of those kids aged between 12 and 15 who are fans of Guns n' Roses might see the ad and think it cool to start smoking! And if two percent of those kids end up dying from lung cancer, then we could have said to be at least partly to blame. That's something I don't want to have responsibility for.
Duff, September 1991

I think that Jimi Hendrix put it best when he said that sometimes the more money you have, the more blues you can sing! I'm serious. I still live life the way I did when I had absolutely no money, but it's nice to have some financial foundations. I do know that now I have a house and a car and I don't have to worry about paying the room service bill. I'm not real frivolous with money. I'm not materialistic.
Slash, June 1992

When you're mother starts wearing Guns T-shirts you know there's something wrong.
Slash, July 1991

It took me a long time to adjust to this place (his new Beverly Hills house). Before this I had an apartment which I got solely because it looked like a hotel room. And I never drove. Now I have two cars in the garage that I never drive either... a 'vette and a Porsche. They're solely for investment purposes. I mean, I got this house because I needed an investment. Which is the most depressing thought. You're buying all this stuff just to sell it when you need to. All the investments I've made are to save my ass when I fuck up.
Slash, February 1991

I'd like to walk away knowing that, like, I can support my kids for whatever they want for the rest of their lives off my interest rates, you know? I'd like to have that security. I've never

We're only as good as our last fucking record, and we're only gonna be as popular as the last album. We're not that important. Because of all the money that's being spent for this little vehicle to happen, we're important. To the business we're important. But if we didn't do this next record, just sit on our asses, we would be forgotten and no-one would care. It's a very temporary thing.
Slash, April 1990

THE FUTURE

I think Guns n' Roses will take it's natural course, even though it could all end tomorrow night. Still, I think we'll take a long break and then come back and do it again. That's what it feels like could happen. But then again, two years ago I never really thought this tour could happen. Frankly, I didn't think any of us would have this much of a future.
Izzy, 1991

I really think that the next official Guns n' Roses record, or the next thing I do at least, will take some dramatic turns that people didn't expect and show the growth. I don't want to be the 23-year-old misfit that I was.
Axl, 1992

Someone recently suggested that I was going to die very soon and I just said to them, 'Yeah, I'm going to die next week, and it'll be on your doorstep!' Sure, Guns n' Roses lives a little bit harder than the rest and there is a self-destructive element about this band. But the will to survive is infinitely stronger... about twice as strong... and that will ensure we're gonna be around for some time to come.
Slash, 1988

When this Guns tour is all over I wanna do something very quickly rather than sit around. I've an idea for a project in my head, a solo album. But whether I do it or not depends on Guns n' Roses. If we go straight into the studio then I won't worry about it. If not then I'll want to keep busy and I'll do something else. What's gonna happen with the next Guns album? We want to keep it real simple, just record nine or ten songs.
Slash, October 1992

WHAT OTHER PEOPLE SAY

In a lot of ways they remind me of the way we were when we were just starting out. They have the choice of how they want to do things though, and there's enough people around for them not to fuck up.
Steven Tyler, Aerosmith, September 1991

What do I think of Guns n' Roses chances of surviving? Hey, it's not my gig to weigh up other people's chances of living or dying, baby... that's what people do to me. I used to be Number One on the list of the next guy to turn into a zero, so I wouldn't dream of doing it to them. I ain't gonna judge 'em... I wish 'em all the luck in the world. They're good guys. What can I tell you? I really feel for those

guys right now 'cos it ain't the Baby Doll Lounge they're playing anymore. Where they're dealing from, it's like Jaws out there every night.
Keith Richards, Rolling Stones, October 1991

A part of me is really pulling for those guys to come through because, Goddammit, right now rock'n'roll desperately needs at least one reasonably young, genuinely charismatic band with real talent, a real sense of what's going on around them and how to express it right, real guts... and who look good. A band who can move the reality of rock'n'roll away from this MTV-era obsessed with ritualised, coiffed bullshit and bring it back home and make it genuinely exciting again.
Iggy Pop, October 1991

To be honest I can understand exactly what Guns n' Roses are doing. They just do what they want to do and they don't give a shit about what the rest of the world thinks. That's the kind of rock'n'roll band I understand!
Angry Anderson, Rose Tattoo, 1989

Touring with Guns n' Roses is like touring with Michael Jackson... although I think I've seen Michael Jackson more times on this tour than I have Axl.
Bill Gould, Faith No More, June 1992

I'm getting more and more confused about who's in Guns n' Roses and it's blowing my mind. There's Dizzy and Iggy and Lizzy and Tizzy and Gilby and Giddy... shit man, onstage now there's a horn section, two chick back-up singers, two keyboard players, an airline pilot, a basketball coach, a coupla car mechanics...
Roddy Bottum, Faith No More, June 1992

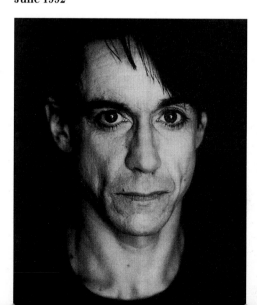